I AM
ALERT
ONLINE

RACHAEL MORLOCK

NEW YORK

Published in 2020 by The Rosen Publishing Group, Inc.
29 East 21st Street, New York, NY 10010

First Edition

Editor: Elizabeth Krajnik
Book Design: Reann Nye

Photo Credits: Cover, pp. 21, 22 wavebreakmedia/Shutterstock.com; p. 5 WeAre/Shutterstock.com; p. 7 Petri Oeschger/Moment/ Getty Images; p. 9 Monkey Business Images/Shutterstock.com; p. 11 Sharaf Maksumov/Shutterstock.com; p. 13 Rawpixel.com/ Shutterstock.com; p. 15 michaeljung/Shutterstock.com; p. 17 Gal Csilla/Shutterstock.com; p. 19 Andrey_Popov/Shutterstock.com.

Cataloging-in-Publication Data

Names: Morlock, Rachael.
Title: I am alert online / Rachael Morlock.
Description: New York : PowerKids Press, 2020. | Series: I am a good digital citizen | Includes glossary and index.
Identifiers: ISBN 9781538349489 (pbk.) | ISBN 9781538349502 (library bound) | ISBN 9781538349496 (6pack)
Subjects: LCSH: Internet and children–Juvenile literature. | Internet–Security measures–Juvenile literature. | Computer crimes–Prevention-
-Juvenile literature.
Classification: LCC HQ784.I58 M67 2020 | DDC 004.67'8083–dc23

Manufactured in the United States of America

CPSIA Compliance Information: Batch #CSPK19. For Further Information contact Rosen Publishing, New York, New York at 1-800-237-9932.

CONTENTS

SHARING THE INTERNET

When you go to a public place, you follow rules. Rules are meant to make things safe and fair for everyone. The Internet is a public place, too! You can be a good digital citizen by following rules and respecting others when you use computers and the Internet.

5

BE ALERT!

One way to be a good digital citizen is to be alert when you use computers. Being alert means watching and understanding your **surroundings**. It means being ready to act. You can be alert online by paying attention to which websites you visit, which people you connect with, and what **information** you share.

ON THE WEB

Billions of people around the world use the Internet. They share information, news, and ideas on many different websites. But not every website is right for you. Teachers and parents can help you find websites that are made just for kids. Whether you're searching for information or playing games, it's important to find the right website.

RELIABLE SITES

Using the right website also means finding one that has **reliable** information. Can you tell the difference between facts and **opinions**? There are good ways to tell if a site is reliable. Check to see if it has an author listed, if the information is recent, if it lists where it got its information, if the site ends with .edu, and if it is free of spelling and grammatical mistakes.

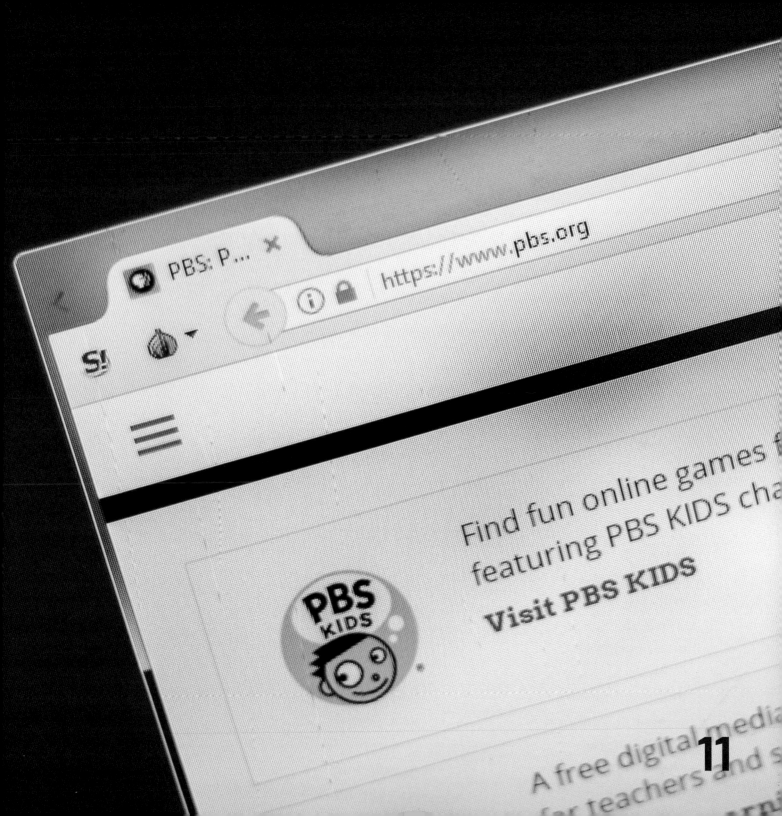

PBS: P...   ×

https://www.pbs.org

Find fun online games f
featuring PBS KIDS cha

Visit PBS KIDS

A free digital media
for teachers and s

11

SHARING INFORMATION

You can find information on many subjects online, but some websites also ask you for information about yourself. You might need to give this information in order to use the site. It's important to be alert when this happens. Make sure to follow your family's or school's rules about sharing information online.

13

PRIVACY

The most important online safety rules are about **privacy**. Information about you, your family members, and your home is private. You should never give others your full name, address, phone number, or birthday without asking for **permission** first. Tell an adult if online strangers or websites ask for private information.

BEWARE OF SCAMS!

Some websites try to catch your attention by offering you prizes. Alert Internet users know that this is a warning sign. A fake offer of prizes is a scam. In return, the website will ask you for money or personal information. You might see scams on websites or in emails.

SAFE AND FUN

Being safe and alert on the Internet can still be fun! You can learn about new subjects, play games, and connect with others. There are many ways to connect without giving away private information. For example, you can create a fun **screen name** that you only share with friends and family.

People

Search

My Status

Games   People   Settings   Help   Sign-Out

My Page
My Friends
My Photos
My Videos
My Groups

Apps
Pages
Interests

Current Name shared a link

Current Name shared a link
That's a cool pic!

Current Name shared a link

Current Name shared a link

PRACTICE AND EXPLORE

It takes practice to be alert online. As you **explore** the Internet, you'll learn to **recognize** different kinds of websites. Whom should you ask if you have questions? What if you feel uncomfortable about what you see online? It's best to talk with a trusted adult when you're unsure.

21

PLAYING YOUR PART

Every digital citizen plays a part in making the Internet a fair, safe, and positive place. When you are alert online, you keep yourself and others safe. You can be alert by paying attention and asking questions. The Internet is always changing, so it's always important to be alert!

GLOSSARY

explore: To search through or look into.

information: Knowledge or facts about something.

opinion: A judgment or belief.

permission: The approval of a person in charge.

privacy: The state of being away from public attention.

recognize: To know and remember upon seeing.

reliable: Trustworthy or dependable.

screen name: The name chosen by a computer user for communicating with others online.

surroundings: The places, conditions, or objects that are around you.

INDEX

A
adult, 14, 20
attention, 16, 22

E
email, 16

F
family, 12, 14, 18
friends, 18

G
games, 8, 18

I
information, 6, 8, 10, 12, 14, 16, 18
Internet, 4, 8, 16, 18, 20, 22

M
money, 16

N
name, 14, 18

P
parents, 8
practice, 20
privacy, 14
prizes, 16

Q
questions, 20, 22

R
rules, 4, 12, 14

S
scam, 16
school, 12
screen name, 18
strangers, 14
surroundings, 6

T
teachers, 8

W
websites, 6, 8, 10, 12, 14, 16, 20

WEBSITES

Due to the changing nature of Internet links, PowerKids Press has developed an online list of websites related to the subject of this book. This site is updated regularly. Please use this link to access the list: www.powerkidslinks.com/digcit/alert